Flat-Out Awesome Knock Knock Jokes For Kids

bob phillips

HARVEST HOUSE PUBLISHERS

EUGENE, OREGON

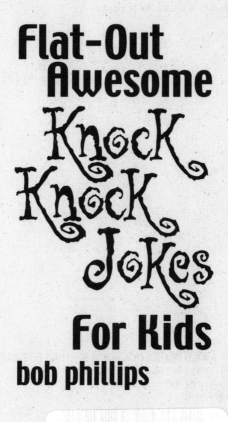

Cover by Dugan Design Group, Bloomington, Minnesota
Cover illustration © Dugan Design Group

FLAT-OUT AWESOME KNOCK-KNOCK JOKES FOR KIDS

Published by Harvest House Publishers
Eugene, Oregon 97402
www.harvesthousepublishers.com

ISBN 978-0-7369-2404-7

Printed in the United States of America

10 11 12 13 14 15 16 / BP-SK / 11 10 9 8 7 6 5

Contents

Stop Knocking on My Door!

Knock, knock.
Who's there?
Aaron.
Aaron who?
Aaron up my tires for a bike ride.

★ ☆ ★

Knock, knock.
Who's there?
Abbie.
Abbie who?
Abbie hive is a dangerous thing to play around.

★ ☆ ★

Knock, knock.
Who's there?
Abyssinia.
Abyssinia who?
Abyssinia later, alligator.

Knock, knock.
Who's there?
Ada.
Ada who?
Ada hot dog at the baseball game.

★ ☆ ★

Knock, knock.
Who's there?
Adam.
Adam who?
Adam is usually made out of cement.

★ ☆ ★

Knock, knock.
Who's there?
Aisle.
Aisle who?
Aisle be knocking on your door every day.

★ ☆ ★

Knock, knock.
Who's there?
Alaska.
Alaska who?
Alaska your mother if you can go swimming with me.

★ ☆ ★

Knock, knock.
Who's there?
Albie.
Albie who?
Albie waiting right here until you open the door.

★ ☆ ★

Knock, knock.
Who's there?
Albion.
Albion who?
Albion my best behavior today.

★ ☆ ★

Knock, knock.
Who's there?
Aleta.
Aleta who?
Aleta big angel food cake all by myself if you don't open the door.

★ ☆ ★

Knock, knock.
Who's there?
Alfie.
Alfie who?
Alfie better when you finally open the door.

★ ☆ ★

Knock, knock.
Who's there?
Alfred.
Alfred who?
Alfred likes to do is ride his skateboard.

★ ☆ ★

Knock, knock.
Who's there?
Allison.
Allison who?
Allison Wonderland is a fun story.

★ ☆ ★

Knock, knock.
Who's there?
Althea.
Althea who?
Althea on the soccer field.

★ ☆ ★

Knock, knock.
Who's there?
Amanda.
Amanda who?
Amanda help rake the leaves would be a good thing.

★ ☆ ★

Somebody Is at the Door!

Knock, knock.
Who's there?
Appeal.
Appeal who?
Appeal is what you get when you are sunburned.

★ ☆ ★

Knock, knock.
Who's there?
Apple.
Apple who?
Apple your leg by telling you another knock-knock joke.

★ ☆ ★

Knock, knock.
Who's there?
Archery.
Archery who?
Archery grows oranges. What grows on your tree?

Knock, knock.
Who's there?
Archibald.
Archibald who?
Archibald because his brother pulled out all his hair.

★ ☆ ★

Knock, knock.
Who's there?
Argue.
Argue who?
Argue going to ever open this door?

★ ☆ ★

Knock, knock.
Who's there?
Arnott.
Arnott who?
Arnott you getting tired of saying who's there?

★ ☆ ★

Knock, knock.
Who's there?
Arthur.
Arthur who?
Arthur any more people in there who can come out and play baseball?

★ ☆ ★

Knock, knock.
Who's there?
Asp.
Asp who?
Stop asping me who's there. Just open the door and let me in.

★ ☆ ★

Knock, knock.
Who's there?
Atmosphere.
Atmosphere who?
Atmosphere is a strange fear of the atmos.

★ ☆ ★

Knock, knock.
Who's there?
Bacon.
Bacon who?
Bacon a cherry pie for your party.

★ ☆ ★

Knock, knock.
Who's there?
Baker.
Baker who?
Baker a nice big cinnamon roll.

★ ☆ ★

Knock, knock.
Who's there?
Banana split.
Banana split who?
Banana split his sides with laughter.

★ ☆ ★

Knock, knock.
Who's there?
Bandage.
Bandage who?
Bandage is when you determine how long a band has been playing.

★ ☆ ★

Knock, knock.
Who's there?
Barked.
Barked who?
Barked my bike in front of your house.

★ ☆ ★

Knock, knock.
Who's there?
Barry.
Barry who?
Barry funny joke, don't you think.

★ ☆ ★

Don't Come In!

Knock, knock.
Who's there?
Beehive.
Beehive who?
Beehive yourself or you'll get into trouble.

★ ☆ ★

Knock, knock.
Who's there?
Beets.
Beets who?
Beets me. I thought you would know the answer.

★ ☆ ★

Knock, knock.
Who's there?
Ben and Anna.
Ben and Anna who?
Sad news…Ben and Anna split.

Knock, knock.
Who's there?
Ben and Doris
Ben and Doris who?
Ben knocking and knocking—I think the Doris stuck.

★ ☆ ★

Knock, knock.
Who's there?
Ben Hur.
Ben Hur who?
Ben Hur a long, long time trying to get your attention.

★ ☆ ★

Knock, knock.
Who's there?
Beth.
Beth who?
Beth of luck to you.

★ ☆ ★

Knock, knock.
Who's there?
Billows.
Billows who?
Billows are something I put on my bed.

★ ☆ ★

Knock, knock.
Who's there?
Billows.
Billows who?
Billows me 50 dollars and I'm here to collect it.

★ ☆ ★

Knock, knock.
Who's there?
Biplane.
Biplane who?
If you don't open the door I'm going home biplane.

★ ☆ ★

Knock, knock.
Who's there?
Bison.
Bison who?
Bison ice cream cones so we can eat them.

★ ☆ ★

Knock, knock.
Who's there?
Blaine.
Blaine who?
I'm always Blained for doing something wrong.

★ ☆ ★

Knock, knock.
Who's there?
Burro.
Burro who?
Can I burro your soccer ball?

★ ☆ ★

Knock, knock.
Who's there?
Butcher.
Butcher who?
Butcher hands up...this is a stickup.

★ ☆ ★

Knock, knock.
Who's there?
Butcher.
Butcher who?
Butcher cuts meat for our family.

★ ☆ ★

Knock, knock.
Who's there?
Butcher.
Butcher who?
Butcher best foot forward.

★ ☆ ★

Who's Outside?

Knock, knock.
Who's there?
Cameron.
Cameron who?
Cameron is what I take pictures with.

★ ☆ ★

Knock, knock.
Who's there?
Canada.
Canada who?
Canada stop with these weird jokes?

★ ☆ ★

Knock, knock.
Who's there?
Candy.
Candy who?
Candy please tell someone else all these jokes?

★ ☆ ★

Knock, knock.
Who's there?
Canoe.
Canoe who?
Canoe believe all of these strange knock-knock jokes?

★ ☆ ★

Knock, knock.
Who's there?
Canter.
Canter who?
Canter you open the door?

★ ☆ ★

Knock, knock.
Who's there?
Canter.
Canter who?
Canter you come out and go for a bike ride?

★ ☆ ★

Knock, knock.
Who's there?
Cantelope.
Cantelope who?
Cantelope without a girlfriend.

★ ☆ ★

Knock, knock.
Who's there?
Carmen.
Carmen who?
Carmen get your hot dog with mustard.

★ ☆ ★

Knock, knock.
Who's there?
Carson.
Carson who?
Carson the garage, and the door is shut.

★ ☆ ★

Knock, knock.
Who's there?
Casual.
Casual who?
I'm moving casual keep forgetting my name.

★ ☆ ★

Knock, knock.
Who's there?
Cat.
Cat who?
Cat play with you right now. I have to mow the lawn.

★ ☆ ★

Knock, knock.
Who's there?
Catcher.
Catcher who?
Catcher before she falls down the stairs!

★ ☆ ★

Knock, knock.
Who's there?
Catsup.
Catsup who?
Catsup in a tree...call the fire department.

★ ☆ ★

Knock, knock.
Who's there?
Cattle.
Cattle who?
Cattle always look for mice.

★ ☆ ★

Knock, knock.
Who's there?
Cauliflower.
Cauliflower who?
Cauliflower if you want a date with a daisy.

★ ☆ ★

Stay Outside!

Knock, knock.
Who's there?
Celeste.
Celeste who?
Celeste time I'm coming to your house.

★ ☆ ★

Knock, knock.
Who's there?
Celeste.
Celeste who?
Celeste time I'm going to tell you a knock-knock joke.

★ ☆ ★

Knock, knock.
Who's there?
Center.
Center who?
Center a message and told her I love her.

Knock, knock.
Who's there?
Chester.
Chester who?
Chester minute more and I'll knock your door down.

★ ☆ ★

Knock, knock.
Who's there?
Coal mine.
Coal mine who?
Coal mine friends and they will tell you who I am.

★ ☆ ★

Knock, knock.
Who's there?
Cod.
Cod who?
Cod a cold and I'm about ready to sneeze.

★ ☆ ★

Knock, knock.
Who's there?
Coffin.
Coffin who?
Coffin a lot because I'm getting a cold out here waiting for you to open the door.

★ ☆ ★

Knock, knock.
Who's there?
Comet.
Comet who?
Comet down a little. I'll tell you if you don't get so excited.

★ ☆ ★

Knock, knock.
Who's there?
Cosmonaut.
Cosmonaut who?
Cosmonaut the one who is doing all the knocking.

★ ☆ ★

Knock, knock.
Who's there?
Cuba.
Cuba who?
Cuba sugar is what you put in your tea.

★ ☆ ★

Knock, knock.
Who's there?
Dancer.
Dancer who?
Dancer the question and you will get a good grade on the test.

★ ☆ ★

Not You Again!

Knock, knock.
Who's there?
Denial.
Denial who?
Denial is a river in Egypt.

★ ☆ ★

Knock, knock.
Who's there?
Denise.
Denise who?
Denise are sore from playing marbles.

★ ☆ ★

Knock, knock.
Who's there?
Dewey.
Dewey who?
Dewey have to hear more of these knock-knock jokes?

Knock, knock.
Who's there?
Diana.
Diana who?
Diana hunger from standing out here so long.

★ ☆ ★

Knock, knock.
Who's there?
Diego.
Diego who?
Diego before de *b*.

★ ☆ ★

Knock, knock.
Who's there?
Diesel.
Diesel who?
Diesel be a funny knock-knock joke.

★ ☆ ★

Knock, knock.
Who's there?
Dinah Snores.
Dinah Snores who?
Dinah Snores have all died off.

★ ☆ ★

Knock, knock.
Who's there?
Disaster.
Disaster who?
Disaster be the worst knock-knock joke I've ever told.

★ ☆ ★

Knock, knock.
Who's there?
Dishes.
Dishes who?
Dishes the last time I'm coming to your house.

★ ☆ ★

Knock, knock.
Who's there?
Dish towel.
Dish towel who?
Dish towel is soaked after falling into the swimming pool.

★ ☆ ★

Knock, knock.
Who's there?
Dismay.
Dismay who?
Dismay is when flowers bloom after April showers.

★ ☆ ★

Knock, knock.
Who's there?
Distress.
Distress who?
Distress makes me look like a hippopotamus in a tutu.

★ ☆ ★

Knock, knock.
Who's there?
Doctor Dolittle.
Doctor Dolittle who?
Doctor Dolittle with my broken finger…it still hurts.

★ ☆ ★

Knock, knock.
Who's there?
Dogma.
Dogma who?
Dogma is the name of a dog's mother.

★ ☆ ★

Knock, knock.
Who's there?
Donna.
Donna who?
Donna you have to finish your homework?

★ ☆ ★

Who Could That Be?

Knock, knock.
Who's there?
Eclipse.
Eclipse who?
Eclipse his toenails with a toenail clipper.

★ ☆ ★

Knock, knock.
Who's there?
Eel.
Eel who?
Eel is what your broken bones do when the doctor puts them into a cast.

★ ☆ ★

Knock, knock.
Who's there?
Egg roll and sausage.
Egg roll and sausage who?
Egg roll off the table and broke—I never sausage a mess.

Knock, knock.
Who's there?
Eggs.
Eggs who?
Eggs it is the door you want to go out of when you're leaving the building.

★ ☆ ★

Knock, knock.
Who's there?
Eileen.
Eileen who?
Eileen on a crutch because I broke my foot.

★ ☆ ★

Knock, knock.
Who's there?
Elaine.
Elaine who?
Elaine down on the job could get you fired.

★ ☆ ★

Knock, knock.
Who's there?
Eli.
Eli who?
Eli to me—he really knows who's there.

★ ☆ ★

Knock, knock.
Who's there?
Ellie Fence.
Ellie Fence who?
Ellie Fence like to eat peanuts.

★ ☆ ★

Knock, knock.
Who's there?
Ellis.
Ellis who?
Ellis the letter that comes after *k*.

★ ☆ ★

Knock, knock.
Who's there?
Elvis.
Elvis who?
Elvis are Santa's helpers at Christmas.

★ ☆ ★

Knock, knock.
Who's there?
Emerson.
Emerson who?
Emerson blue eyes you have.

★ ☆ ★

Knock, knock.
Who's there?
Enid.
Enid who?
Enid help with all these packages I'm carrying.

★ ☆ ★

Knock, knock.
Who's there?
Esau.
Esau who?
Esau you look out the window to see who it was.

★ ☆ ★

Knock, knock.
Who's there?
Esther.
Esther who?
Esther anybody who will answer the door?

★ ☆ ★

Knock, knock.
Who's there?
Esther.
Esther who?
Esther another way to get you to open the door without knocking?

★ ☆ ★

What's That Noise?

Knock, knock.
Who's there?
Feline
Feline who?
Feline good after I got an *A* on the test.

★ ☆ ★

Knock, knock.
Who's there?
Ferris.
Ferris who?
The Ferris a fun place. You wanna go?

★ ☆ ★

Knock, knock.
Who's there?
Fido.
Fido who?
Fido known you weren't going to open the door, I wouldn't have come.

★ ☆ ★

Knock, knock.
Who's there?
Filler.
Filler who?
Filler up—my gas tank is empty.

★ ☆ ★

Knock, knock.
Who's there?
Flora.
Flora who?
Flora my house got wet when the water pipe burst.

★ ☆ ★

Knock, knock.
Who's there?
Foremen.
Foremen who?
Formen fell down laughing at my knock-knock joke.

★ ☆ ★

Knock, knock.
Who's there?
Foremen.
Foremen who?
Foremen ran away. They didn't want to hear any more jokes.

★ ☆ ★

Knock, knock.
Who's there?
Freeze.
Freeze who?
"Freeze a Jolly Good Fellow" is a song Frosty the Snowman sings to Santa Claus.

★ ☆ ★

Knock, knock.
Who's there?
Freezing.
Freezing who?
I'll keep freezing out here until you open the door.

★ ☆ ★

Knock, knock.
Who's there?
Galahad.
Galahad who?
Galahad a bike until it was stolen.

★ ☆ ★

Knock, knock.
Who's there?
Gallop.
Gallop who?
Gallop down some soda pop with me.

★ ☆ ★

Who Keeps Knocking on My Door?

Knock, knock.
Who's there?
Gopher.
Gopher who?
Gopher the key and unlock the door.

★ ☆ ★

Knock, knock.
Who's there?
Gopher.
Gopher who?
Gopher a walk with me today.

★ ☆ ★

Knock, knock.
Who's there?
Gorilla.
Gorilla who?
Gorilla is what I cook hamburgers on.

Knock, knock.
Who's there?
Grover.
Grover who?
She plans to grover hair longer.

★ ☆ ★

Knock, knock.
Who's there?
Gruesome.
Gruesome who?
You're taller. It looks like you gruesome.

★ ☆ ★

Knock, knock.
Who's there?
Gumby.
Gumby who?
Gumby very hard to scrape off of your shoe.

★ ☆ ★

Knock, knock.
Who's there?
Guru.
Guru who?
Guru six inches since I last saw you.

★ ☆ ★

Knock, knock.
Who's there?
Gus.
Gus who?
Gus I'll have to try someone else's door.

★ ☆ ★

Knock, knock.
Who's there?
Gwen.
Gwen who?
Gwen to the computer store. Want to come?

★ ☆ ★

Knock, knock.
Who's there?
Halibut.
Halibut who?
Halibut opening the door—I'm tired of knocking

★ ☆ ★

Knock, knock.
Who's there?
Hammer.
Hammer who?
Hammer eggs make a Denver omelet.

★ ☆ ★

Knock, knock.
Who's there?
Hank.
Hank who?
Hank you for finally opening the door.

★ ☆ ★

Knock, knock.
Who's there?
Hank.
Hank who?
You're welcome.

★ ☆ ★

Knock, knock.
Who's there?
Hans.
Hans who?
Hans off my candy bar.

★ ☆ ★

Knock, knock.
Who's there?
Hardy.
Hardy who?
Hardy-har-har. Isn't this a funny joke?

★ ☆ ★

I Can't Come to the Door!

Knock, knock.
Who's there?
Hatch-hatch-hatch.
Hatch-hatch-hatch who?
Do you have a cold?

★ ☆ ★

Knock, knock.
Who's there?
Hayes.
Hayes who?
Hayes what donkeys eat.

★ ☆ ★

Knock, knock.
Who's there?
Hawaii.
Hawaii who?
I'm fine. Hawaii you?

Knock, knock.
Who's there?
Heaven.
Heaven who?
Heaven we met here before?

★ ☆ ★

Knock, knock.
Who's there?
Helmet.
Helmet who?
Helmet is what I wear when I ride my bike.

★ ☆ ★

Knock, knock.
Who's there?
Henrietta.
Henrietta who?
Henrietta worm and got sick.

★ ☆ ★

Knock, knock.
Who's there?
Herring.
Herring who?
Herring aids can help you to hear people talk.

★ ☆ ★

Knock, knock.
Who's there?
Hogwash.
Hogwash who?
Hogwash is what dirty pigs do to get clean.

★ ☆ ★

Knock, knock.
Who's there?
Homer.
Homer who?
Homer is what baseball players like to hit.

★ ☆ ★

Knock, knock.
Who's there?
Honeycomb.
Honeycomb who?
Honeycomb your hair before work—this is your mother.

★ ☆ ★

Knock, knock.
Who's there?
Howie.
Howie who?
I'm fine—Howie you?

★ ☆ ★

Knock, knock.
Who's there?
Howie.
Howie who?
Howie doing? Do you want to hear more knock-knock jokes?

★ ☆ ★

Knock, knock.
Who's there?
Howie.
Howie who?
Howie forget so quickly who's there I'll never understand.

★ ☆ ★

Knock, knock.
Who's there?
Hugh.
Hugh who?
Hugh who to you too.

★ ☆ ★

Knock, knock.
Who's there?
Hugh.
Hugh who?
Hugh are so funny.

★ ☆ ★

Come Back Tomorrow!

Knock, knock.
Who's there?
Icon.
Icon who?
Icon tell more knock-knock jokes than you can.

★ ☆ ★

Knock, knock.
Who's there?
Ida.
Ida who?
Ida like to know why you don't answer the door.

★ ☆ ★

Knock, knock.
Who's there?
Iguana.
Iguana who?
Iguana hold your hand.

★ ☆ ★

Knock, knock.
Who's there?
Imus.
Imus who?
Imus stop telling knock-knock jokes before I lose my mind.

★ ☆ ★

Knock, knock.
Who's there?
India.
India who?
India meantime, I'll tell someone else these jokes.

★ ☆ ★

Knock, knock.
Who's there?
Intense.
Intense who?
Intense circumstances such as these, I tell jokes.

★ ☆ ★

Knock, knock.
Who's there?
Iran.
Iran who?
Iran a long way to see you.

★ ☆ ★

Knock, knock.
Who's there?
Iran
Iran who?
Iran a long ways to get your attention.

★ ☆ ★

Knock, knock.
Who's there?
Iran
Iran who?
Iran as fast as I could to get away from the last person I told this joke to.

★ ☆ ★

Knock, knock.
Who's there?
Irene.
Irene who?
Irene the doorbell but it must be broken…that's why I knocked.

★ ☆ ★

Knock, knock.
Who's there?
Isadore.
Isadore who?
Isadore ever going to be opened?

★ ☆ ★

Knock, knock.
Who's there?
Isadore.
Isadore who?
Isadore always closed like this?

★ ☆ ★

Knock, knock.
Who's there?
Island.
Island who?
Island on my feet whenever I slip off your porch.

★ ☆ ★

Knock, knock.
Who's there?
Island.
Island who?
Island on my head when I fell off my skateboard.

★ ☆ ★

Knock, knock.
Who's there?
Ivanna.
Ivanna who?
Ivanna hold your hand.

★ ☆ ★

You've Got the Wrong House!

Knock, knock.
Who's there?
Jamaica.
Jamaica who?
Jamaica up all of the knock-knock jokes yourself?

★ ☆ ★

Knock, knock.
Who's there?
Jeannie.
Jeannie who?
Jeannie is something you let out of a magic lantern.

★ ☆ ★

Knock, knock.
Who's there?
Jerome.
Jerome who?
You can get into trouble if Jerome around the classroom during a test.

Knock, knock.
Who's there?
Jester.
Jester who?
Jester forget it. I don't want to come in now.

★ ☆ ★

Knock, knock.
Who's there?
Jewel.
Jewel who?
Jewel find the answer when you open the door.

★ ☆ ★

Knock, knock.
Who's there?
Juan.
Juan who?
Juan day you will feel guilty and open the door.

★ ☆ ★

Knock, knock.
Who's there?
Julie.
Julie who?
Julie comes before August and September.

★ ☆ ★

Knock, knock.
Who's there?
Juliet.
Juliet who?
Juliet all of my candy.

★ ☆ ★

Knock, knock.
Who's there?
July.
July who?
July…you really know who is knocking.

★ ☆ ★

Knock, knock.
Who's there?
Juno.
Juno who?
Juno any other knock-knock jokes?

★ ☆ ★

Knock, knock.
Who's there?
Jupiter.
Jupiter who?
Jupiter tennis shoes on and went for a walk.

★ ☆ ★

Knock, knock.
Who's there?
Justin.
Justin who?
You're Justin time to open the door.

★ ☆ ★

Knock, knock.
Who's there?
Kanga.
Kanga who?
No, it's not Kangawho—it's Kangaroo.

★ ☆ ★

Knock, knock.
Who's there?
Keith.
Keith who?
Keith me on the lips, sweetheart.

★ ☆ ★

Knock, knock.
Who's there?
Kelp.
Kelp who?
Kelp me! I think I'm drowning!

★ ☆ ★

Knock It Off!

Knock, knock.
Who's there?
Kerry.
Kerry who?
Kerry my books for me, please.

★ ☆ ★

Knock, knock.
Who's there?
Kiefer.
Kiefer who?
Kiefer my door fell down the sewer.

★ ☆ ★

Knock, knock.
Who's there?
Kimmy.
Kimmy who?
Kimmy a piece of bubble gum.

Knock, knock.
Who's there?
Kip.
Kip who?
Kip answering who's there—I love telling knock-knock jokes.

★ ☆ ★

Knock, knock.
Who's there?
Kipper.
Kipper who?
Kipper locked up in the zoo for people to look at.

★ ☆ ★

Knock, knock.
Who's there?
Kipper.
Kipper who?
Kipper silly knock-knock jokes to yourself.

★ ☆ ★

Knock, knock.
Who's there?
Kitty litter.
Kitty litter who?
Kitty litter kittens play outside on the grass.

★ ☆ ★

Knock, knock.
Who's there?
Kleenex.
Kleenex who?
Your Kleenex looks better now that you've washed.

★ ☆ ★

Knock, knock.
Who's there?
Krakatoa.
Krakatoa who?
Krakatoa when I kicked your door.

★ ☆ ★

Knock, knock.
Who's there?
Kumquat.
Kumquat who?
Kumquat-ly while they take you away to the loony farm.

★ ☆ ★

Knock, knock.
Who's there?
Lady.
Lady who?
Lady down on the floor laughing at all these jokes.

★ ☆ ★

Knock, knock.
Who's there?
Landon.
Landon who?
Landon on your bottom doesn't feel good.

★ ☆ ★

Knock, knock.
Who's there?
Laurel.
Laurel who?
Laurel is what they sometimes make wreaths out of.

★ ☆ ★

Knock, knock.
Who's there?
Leda.
Leda who?
Leda me to the back door—maybe it's open.

★ ☆ ★

Knock, knock.
Who's there?
Lego.
Lego who?
Lego of the door handle so I can come in.

★ ☆ ★

To Open or Not to Open...

Knock, knock.
Who's there?
Linda.
Linda who?
Linda me some sugar so I can bake a cake.

★ ☆ ★

Knock, knock.
Who's there?
Lisa.
Lisa who?
Lisa know you care who's outside.

★ ☆ ★

Knock, knock.
Who's there?
Liver.
Liver who?
Liver alone...she's not bothering you.

Knock, knock.
Who's there?
Liver.
Liver who?
Liver up and have a good time.

★ ☆ ★

Knock, knock.
Who's there?
Lizard.
Lizard who?
Lizard that you wanted me to come over to your house...so here I am.

★ ☆ ★

Knock, knock.
Who's there?
Luke.
Luke who?
Luke out the window, silly...then you'll know who's there.

★ ☆ ★

Knock, knock.
Who's there?
Luke.
Luke who?
Luke up my name in the phone book and then you'll know.

★ ☆ ★

Knock, knock.

Who's there?

Luther.

Luther who?

The luther my pants are, the more likely they'll fall down.

★ ☆ ★

Knock, knock.

Who's there?

Mabel.

Mabel who?

Mabel I'll go knock on someone else's door.

★ ☆ ★

Knock, knock.

Who's there?

Macaw.

Macaw who?

Macaw ran out of gas.

★ ☆ ★

Knock, knock.

Who's there?

Mackie.

Mackie who?

I really like Mackie roni and cheese.

★ ☆ ★

Knock, knock.
Who's there?
Major.
Major who?
Major day by telling you a knock-knock joke, didn't I?

★ ☆ ★

Knock, knock.
Who's there?
Major.
Major who?
Major come to the door.

★ ☆ ★

Knock, knock.
Who's there?
Mango.
Mango who?
Mango work in the office.

★ ☆ ★

Knock, knock.
Who's there?
Marcus.
Marcus who?
Marcus waiting for you to come out and play.

★ ☆ ★

Too Many Knock-Knock Jokes!

Knock, knock.
Who's there?
Melbourne.
Melbourne who?
Melbourne on Tuesday the twenty-first...when were you born?

★ ☆ ★

Knock, knock.
Who's there?
Midas.
Midas who?
Midas well tell you another knock-knock joke.

★ ☆ ★

Knock, knock.
Who's there?
Milton.
Milton who?
Milton my ice cream cone waiting for you to open the door.

Knock, knock.
Who's there?
Mission.
Mission who?
Mission you less and less the more you tell knock-knock jokes.

★ ☆ ★

Knock, knock.
Who's there?
Missouri.
Missouri who?
Missouri loves company.

★ ☆ ★

Knock, knock.
Who's there?
Morrie.
Morrie who?
Morrie tells knock-knock jokes, the sicker I feel.

★ ☆ ★

Knock, knock.
Who's there?
Mustard.
Mustard who?
Mustard left my glasses at your house.

★ ☆ ★

Knock, knock.
Who's there?
Myth.
Myth who?
Myth my two fwont teefth for Christmoth.

★ ☆ ★

Knock, knock.
Who's there?
Nadia.
Nadia who?
Nadia head if you know who is at the door.

★ ☆ ★

Knock, knock.
Who's there?
Nanny.
Nanny who?
Nanny, Nanny, Nanny…I'm not going to tell you.

★ ☆ ★

Knock, knock.
Who's there?
Napkin.
Napkin who?
Napkin help you out when you are tired.

★ ☆ ★

Knock, knock.
Who's there?
Needle.
Needle who?
Needle help with this door…it won't open.

★ ☆ ★

Knock, knock.
Who's there?
Nickel.
Nickel who?
Nickel be coming over to play with us.

★ ☆ ★

Knock, knock.
Who's there?
Nickel.
Nickel who?
Nickel get an ax and chop down your door if you don't open it.

★ ☆ ★

Knock, knock.
Who's there?
Noah.
Noah who?
Noah any more knock-knock jokes?

★ ☆ ★

Hold On! I'm on My Way!

Knock, knock.
Who's there?
Norway.
Norway who?
Norway am I going to tell you.

★ ☆ ★

Knock, knock.
Who's there?
Ohio.
Ohio who?
Ohio, heigh ho, it's off to work we go.

★ ☆ ★

Knock, knock.
Who's there?
Oil.
Oil who?
Oil see you later, alligator.

Knock, knock.
Who's there?
Oink-oink.
Oink-oink who?
Let me guess. You're part pig and part owl.

★ ☆ ★

Knock, knock.
Who's there?
Olaf.
Olaf who?
Olaf out loud at all of these jokes.

★ ☆ ★

Knock, knock.
Who's there?
Olive.
Olive who?
Olive around the corner on the next block.

★ ☆ ★

Knock, knock.
Who's there?
Oliver.
Oliver who?
Oliver is what people who like liver say before they eat it.

★ ☆ ★

Knock, knock.
Who's there?
Oliver.
Oliver who?
Oliver friends went home. She's the only one still knocking.

★ ☆ ★

Knock, knock.
Who's there?
Orange.
Orange who?
Orange you tired of all these knock-knock jokes?

★ ☆ ★

Knock, knock.
Who's there?
Orbit.
Orbit who?
Orbit of a strange person.

★ ☆ ★

Knock, knock.
Who's there?
Osborn.
Osborn who?
Osborn on Christmas. When were you born?

★ ☆ ★

Knock, knock.
Who's there?
Oslo.
Oslo who?
Oslo down after running a mile.

★ ☆ ★

Knock, knock.
Who's there?
Ostrich.
Ostrich who?
Ostrich my arms when I wake up in the morning.

★ ☆ ★

Knock, knock.
Who's there?
Oswald.
Oswald who?
Oswald my gum when I saw the teacher coming.

★ ☆ ★

Knock, knock.
Who's there?
Oswald.
Oswald who?
Oswald a fly and it bugs me.

★ ☆ ★

I Won't Open the Door!

Knock, knock.
Who's there?
Panther.
Panther who?
Panther all dirty from playing in the mud.

★ ☆ ★

Knock, knock.
Who's there?
Panther.
Panther who?
My panther falling down because I don't have a belt.

★ ☆ ★

Knock, knock.
Who's there?
Paradise.
Paradise who?
Paradise is what you roll when you play Monopoly.

Knock, knock.
Who's there?
Paradox.
Paradox who?
Paradox is simply two doctors.

★ ☆ ★

Knock, knock.
Who's there?
Parka.
Parka who?
Parka your bike next to the tree on the front lawn.

★ ☆ ★

Knock, knock.
Who's there?
Pasta.
Pasta who?
Pasta chocolate cake and ice cream.

★ ☆ ★

Knock, knock.
Who's there?
Pencil.
Pencil who?
Pencil keep falling down…I think I need a belt.

★ ☆ ★

Knock, knock.
Who's there?
Pecan.
Pecan who?
Pecan your window to see if you're there.

★ ☆ ★

Knock, knock.
Who's there?
Peeka.
Peeka who?
No, no. Peekaboo, not peeka who.

★ ☆ ★

Knock, knock.
Who's there?
Phyllis.
Phyllis who?
Phyllis up—my car is out of gas.

★ ☆ ★

Knock, knock.
Who's there?
Pickle.
Pickle who?
Pickle break the hard ground better than your shovel.

★ ☆ ★

Knock, knock.
Who's there?
Picture.
Picture who?
Picture door out and thought I'd knock on it.

★ ☆ ★

Knock, knock.
Who's there?
Pike.
Pike who?
Pike riding is like bike riding—only fish like to do it.

★ ☆ ★

Knock, knock.
Who's there?
Pink panther.
Pink panther who?
Pink panther not what boys wear.

★ ☆ ★

Knock, knock.
Who's there?
Pitcher.
Pitcher who?
Pitcher Sunday best on, and we can walk to church this morning.

★ ☆ ★

All That Knocking Is Giving Me a Headache!

Knock, knock.
Who's there?
Police.
Police who?
Police to finally meet you.

★ ☆ ★

Knock, knock.
Who's there?
Poodle.
Poodle who?
Poodle little love in your heart.

★ ☆ ★

Knock, knock.
Who's there?
Poster.
Poster who?
Poster remember who's there.

Knock, knock.
Who's there?
Pressure.
Pressure who?
Pressure eye up to the keyhole and look out...then you'll know.

★ ☆ ★

Knock, knock.
Who's there?
Pudding.
Pudding who?
I'm pudding you on with all these knock-knock jokes.

★ ☆ ★

Knock, knock.
Who's there?
Pudding.
Pudding who?
Pudding your hand into a light socket is really dumb.

★ ☆ ★

Knock, knock.
Who's there?
Pullover.
Pullover who?
Pullover quick...I think I'm getting sick.

★ ☆ ★

Knock, knock.
Who's there?
Punch.
Punch who?
Punch anyone you want except me.

★ ☆ ★

Knock, knock.
Who's there?
Pushkin.
Pushkin who?
Pushkin the lawn mower makes me tired.

★ ☆ ★

Knock, knock.
Who's there?
Pushkin.
Pushkin who?
Pushkin people around is not a good idea.

★ ☆ ★

Knock, knock.
Who's there?
Pushkin.
Pushkin who?
Pushkin knock-knock jokes on people is dangerous.

★ ☆ ★

Knock, knock.
Who's there?
Quacker.
Quacker who?
Quacker cwumbs are what ducks make when they eat.

★ ☆ ★

Knock, knock.
Who's there?
Quack.
Quack who?
Quack my tooth on a popcorn seed.

★ ☆ ★

Knock, knock.
Who's there?
Queen.
Queen who?
Queen up your room or you'll get into trouble.

★ ☆ ★

Knock, knock.
Who's there?
Queue.
Queue who?
Queue better open the door or I'll huff and puff and blow it down.

★ ☆ ★

Stop Beating the Door!

Knock, knock.
Who's there?
Raptor.
Raptor who?
She raptor hula hoop around her hips

★ ☆ ★

Knock, knock.
Who's there?
Rat.
Rat who?
Rat-a-tat goes the woodpecker.

★ ☆ ★

Knock, knock.
Who's there?
Raisin.
Raisin who?
Raisin chickens is a cheep-cheep paying job.

Knock, knock.
Who's there?
Razor.
Razor who?
Razor window and look and see who it is.

★ ☆ ★

Knock, knock.
Who's there?
Reindeer.
Reindeer who?
Reindeer…that's why it's too wet to play outside.

★ ☆ ★

Knock, knock.
Who's there?
Rhubarb.
Rhubarb who?
Rhubarb is a sharp object on the 'rhu' plant.

★ ☆ ★

Knock, knock.
Who's there?
Ringo.
Ringo who?
Ringo on the finger…not in your nose.

★ ☆ ★

Knock, knock.
Who's there?
Robin.
Robin who?
Robin people will end up getting you thrown into jail.

★ ☆ ★

Knock, knock.
Who's there?
Rocco.
Rocco who?
Rocco-bye baby, on the treetop…

★ ☆ ★

Knock, knock.
Who's there?
Rocket.
Rocket who?
I like to sit in the chair on your porch and rocket.

★ ☆ ★

Knock, knock.
Who's there?
Ron.
Ron who?
Ron fast and open the door.

★ ☆ ★

Knock, knock.
Who's there?
Russian.
Russian who?
Russian around the neighborhood and trying to get someone to open the door.

★ ☆ ★

Knock, knock.
Who's there?
Sabine.
Sabine who?
Sabine knocking on this door for a long, long time.

★ ☆ ★

Knock, knock.
Who's there?
Saddle.
Saddle who?
Saddle up your horse and let's go for a ride.

★ ☆ ★

Knock, knock.
Who's there?
Sadie.
Sadie who?
Sadie magic word and I'll tell you who I am.

★ ☆ ★

Knock, knock.
Who's there?
Salad.
Salad who?
Salad a wonderful time at your party.

★ ☆ ★

Knock, knock.
Who's there?
Sally.
Sally who?
I feel really Sally telling you all these knock-knock jokes.

★ ☆ ★

Knock, knock.
Who's there?
Salmon.
Salmon who?
Salmon chanted evening you may meet a stranger.

★ ☆ ★

Knock, knock.
Who's there?
Samoa.
Samoa who?
I would like Samoa ice cream, please.

What's That Drumming Sound?

Knock, knock.
Who's there?
Samson.
Samson who?
Samson is looking for his father.

★ ☆ ★

Knock, knock.
Who's there?
Sandal.
Sandal who?
Sandal get into my swimming suit if I swim in the ocean.

★ ☆ ★

Knock, knock.
Who's there?
Sarah.
Sarah who?
Sarah doctor in the house? These jokes are making me ill.

Knock, knock.
Who's there?
Sandy.
Sandy who?
Sandy Claus brings presents on Christmas.

★ ☆ ★

Knock, knock.
Who's there?
Sasha.
Sasha who?
Sasha funny knock-knock joke.

★ ☆ ★

Knock, knock.
Who's there?
Say.
Say who?
Who.

★ ☆ ★

Knock, knock.
Who's there?
Selma.
Selma who?
Selma old soccer ball for $5.00.

★ ☆ ★

Knock, knock.
Who's there?
Senior.
Senior who?
Senior weird brother walking down the street.

★ ☆ ★

Knock, knock.
Who's there?
Scold.
Scold who?
Scold out here—let me in.

★ ☆ ★

Knock, knock.
Who's there?
Scolder.
Scolder who?
The longer you wait the scolder it is getting out here.

★ ☆ ★

Knock, knock.
Who's there?
Scott.
Scott who?
You've Scott to stop telling these jokes.

★ ☆ ★

Knock, knock.
Who's there?
Sharon.
Sharon who?
Sharon your toys is a polite thing to do.

★ ☆ ★

Knock, knock.
Who's there?
Shellfish.
Shellfish who?
Shellfish people only think about themselves and won't answer the door.

★ ☆ ★

Knock, knock.
Who's there?
Sherwood.
Sherwood who?
Sherwood like to have you stop telling knock-knock jokes.

★ ☆ ★

Knock, knock.
Who's there?
Shirley.
Shirley who?
Shirley you must know who it is.

★ ☆ ★

Knock, knock.
Who's there?
Should hold.
Should hold who?
Should hold acquaintance be forgot…

★ ☆ ★

Knock, knock.
Who's there?
Snapper.
Snapper who?
Snapper fingers and I'll come running.

★ ☆ ★

Please, No More Knock-Knock Jokes!

Knock, knock.
Who's there?
Sonia.
Sonia who?
Sonia matter of time before I kick the door down.

★ ☆ ★

Knock, knock.
Who's there?
Spell.
Spell who?
W–H–O.

★ ☆ ★

Knock, knock.
Who's there?
Statue.
Statue who?
Statue with the funny face?

Knock, knock.
Who's there?
Sweater.
Sweater who?
Sweater is what they call someone who works hard on a hot day.

★ ☆ ★

Knock, knock.
Who's there?
Selma.
Selma who?
Selma house and move if you don't open the door.

★ ☆ ★

Knock, knock.
Who's there?
Settler.
Settler who?
Settler down—she's acting silly again.

★ ☆ ★

Knock, knock.
Who's there?
Shaker.
Shaker who?
Shaker is something you get salt and pepper out of.

★ ☆ ★

Knock, knock.
Who's there?
Shaker.
Shaker who?
Shaker hard…she'll miss the school bus if she doesn't get up.

★ ☆ ★

Knock, knock.
Who's there?
Shalt not.
Shalt not who?
It's a new commandment: "Thou shalt not tell anymore knock-knock jokes."

★ ☆ ★

Knock, knock.
Who's there?
Sharon.
Sharon who?
Sharon good times with friends is fun.

★ ☆ ★

Knock, knock.
Who's there?
Shaver.
Shaver who?
Shaver jokes for later.

★ ☆ ★

Knock, knock.
Who's there?
Sheila.
Sheila who?
Sheila cry if you don't open the door.

★ ☆ ★

Knock, knock.
Who's there?
Sheila.
Sheila who?
Sheila be coming around the mountain when she comes.

★ ☆ ★

Knock, knock.
Who's there?
Shelby.
Shelby who?
Shelby going shopping without you.

★ ☆ ★

Knock, knock.
Who's there?
Sherbet.
Sherbet who?
Sherbet is when you make a wager on something that is guaranteed to happen.

★ ☆ ★

Knock, knock.
Who's there?
Sherwood.
Sherwood who?
Sherwood appreciate it if you would open the door.

★ ☆ ★

Knock, knock.
Who's there?
Sherwood.
Sherwood who?
Sherwood dance for joy if you would stop telling knock-knock jokes.

★ ☆ ★

Knock, knock.
Who's there?
Shirley.
Shirley who?
Shirley you must be joking…you know who I am.

★ ☆ ★

Knock, knock.
Who's there?
Shortstop.
Shortstop who?
A shortstop is when you do not remain long at a stop sign.

★ ☆ ★

Knock, knock.
Who's there?
Shuttle.
Shuttle who?
Shuttle the windows—the wind is starting to blow.

★ ☆ ★

Knock, knock.
Who's there?
Skidoo.
Skidoo who?
Skid–"oo" is a noise you make when you skid and are about to fall down.

★ ☆ ★

Knock, knock.
Who's there?
Slap-a-doodle.
Slap-a-doodle who?
Are you a rooster?

★ ☆ ★

Knock, knock.
Who's there?
Snot.
Snot who?
Snot any of your business.

★ ☆ ★

Knock, knock.
Who's there?
Snot.
Snot who?
Your joke snot funny.

★ ☆ ★

Knock, knock.
Who's there?
Spider.
Spider who?
Spider on the football field doing her cheerleading.

★ ☆ ★

Knock, knock.
Who's there?
Splinter.
Splinter who?
Splinter in my finger. Can I borrow your tweasers?

★ ☆ ★

Knock, knock.
Who's there?
Stella.
Stella who?
Stella standing here waiting for you to open up.

★ ☆ ★

Knock, knock.
Who's there?
Stella.
Stella who?
Stella telling these crazy knock-knock jokes.

★ ☆ ★

Knock, knock.
Who's there?
Suture.
Suture who?
Suture self—I'll be knocking on someone else's door.

★ ☆ ★

Knock, knock.
Who's there?
Sweden.
Sweden who?
Sweden sour is a sauce you eat at Chinese restaurants.

★ ☆ ★

Knock, knock.
Who's there?
Talia.
Talia who?
Talia another knock-knock joke if you like.

★ ☆ ★

Knock, knock.
Who's there?
Tamara.
Tamara who?
Tamara is Monday and I have to go to school.

★ ☆ ★

Knock, knock.
Who's there?
Tanks.
Tanks who?
Tanks for asking.

★ ☆ ★

Knock, knock.
Who's there?
Tanks.
Tanks who?
Tanks for the memory...

★ ☆ ★

Knock, knock.
Who's there?
Tanks.
Tanks who?
Tanks for listening to all my knock-knock jokes.

★ ☆ ★

Knock, knock.
Who's there?
Tara.
Tara who?
Tara down the stairs and open the door.

★ ☆ ★

Knock, knock.
Who's there?
Teddy bear.
Teddy bear who?
Teddy bear because he doesn't have any clothes.

★ ☆ ★

Knock, knock.
Who's there?
Tennis.
Tennis who?
Tennis when I start to get tired and want to go to bed.

★ ☆ ★

Knock, knock.
Who's there?
Terrace.
Terrace who?
Terrace a big hole in my pants.

★ ☆ ★

No More Silly Visitors!

Knock, knock.
Who's there?
Therese.
Therese who?
Therese got to be an end to these jokes.

★ ☆ ★

Knock, knock.
Who's there?
Thesis.
Thesis who?
Thesis another wacky knock-knock joke.

★ ☆ ★

Knock, knock.
Who's there?
Throat.
Throat who?
If you want to play ball, just throat to me.

Knock, knock.
Who's there?
Thumb.
Thumb who?
Thumb thing is very loony about this joke.

★ ☆ ★

Knock, knock.
Who's there?
Thumping.
Thumping who?
Thumping tells me we're getting to the end of these knock-knock jokes.

★ ☆ ★

Knock, knock.
Who's there?
Tibet.
Tibet who?
Tibet and lose money is not a good thing.

★ ☆ ★

Knock, knock.
Who's there?
Tidal.
Tidal who?
I tidal his shoelaces together—watch what happens.

★ ☆ ★

Knock, knock.
Who's there?
Tilda.
Tilda who?
Tilda door opens, the knocking will continue.

★ ☆ ★

Knock, knock.
Who's there?
Tom Sawyer.
Tom Sawyer who?
Tom Sawyer looking out the window.

★ ☆ ★

Knock, knock.
Who's there?
Toucan
Toucan who?
Toucan have a good time playing together.

★ ☆ ★

Knock, knock.
Who's there?
Treble.
Treble who?
Treble with you is that you never open the door.

★ ☆ ★

Knock, knock.
Who's there?
Tuba.
Tuba who?
I squeeze the tuba toothpaste in the middle.

★ ☆ ★

Knock, knock.
Who's there?
Tulips.
Tulips who?
Tulips are what you need when kissing.

★ ☆ ★

Knock, knock.
Who's there?
Tuna.
Tuna who?
Tuna your tuba. You're killing me with the noise.

★ ☆ ★

Knock, knock.
Who's there?
Tune
Tune who?
Tune in next time for some more exciting knock-knock jokes!

★ ☆ ★

Stop This Constant Knocking!

Knock, knock.
Who's there?
Ubangi.
Ubangi who?
Ubangi on my door one more time and I'll knock your block off.

★ ☆ ★

Knock, knock.
Who's there?
Udder.
Udder who?
Udder no circumstances tell me another knock-knock joke.

★ ☆ ★

Knock, knock.
Who's there?
Udder disaster.
Udder disaster who?
Udder disaster is what happens when a cow has very short legs.

★ ☆ ★

Knock, knock.
Who's there?
Udder.
Udder who?
Udder-ly ridiculous is what these jokes are.

★ ☆ ★

Knock, knock.
Who's there?
Uganda.
Uganda who?
Uganda a lot of weight after eating all that pizza.

★ ☆ ★

Knock, knock.
Who's there?
Uma.
Uma who?
Uma best friend if you open the door.

★ ☆ ★

Knock, knock.
Who's there?
Urchin.
Urchin who?
Urchin has whiskers on it and needs to be shaved.

★ ☆ ★

Knock, knock.
Who's there?
Uriah.
Uriah who?
Uriah's look cross-eyed.

★ ☆ ★

Knock, knock.
Who's there?
Usher.
Usher who?
Usher up...you talk to much.

★ ☆ ★

Knock, knock.
Who's there?
Vanessa.
Vanessa who?
Vanessa someone going to open the door?

★ ☆ ★

Knock, knock.
Who's there?
Venice.
Venice who?
Venice the movie going to start?

★ ☆ ★

Knock, knock.
Who's there?
Venice.
Venice who?
Venice time to hear the final knock-knock joke? I hope it's soon.

★ ☆ ★

Knock, knock.
Who's there?
Vera.
Vera who?
Vera funny joke...don't you think?

★ ☆ ★

Knock, knock.
Who's there?
Viper.
Viper who?
Viper nose...it's running.

★ ☆ ★

Knock, knock.
Who's there?
Vlad.
Vlad who?
Vlad that these jokes are almost over.

★ ☆ ★

Knock, knock.
Who's there?
Voodoo.
Voodoo who?
Voodoo you think you are—the door monitor?

★ ☆ ★

Knock, knock.
Who's there?
Waddle.
Waddle who?
Waddle out of your chair and open the door.

★ ☆ ★

Knock, knock.
Who's there?
Wanda.
Wanda who?
Wanda come outside and play?

★ ☆ ★

Knock, knock.
Who's there?
Water.
Water who?
Water you waiting for…open the door.

★ ☆ ★

Knock, knock.
Who's there?
Water wings.
Water wings who?
Water wings are what we put on our seaplanes.

★ ☆ ★

Knock, knock.
Who's there?
Wayne.
Wayne who?
Wayne drops keep falling on my head…

★ ☆ ★

Knock, knock.
Who's there?
Weasel.
Weasel who?
Weasel a happy tune.

★ ☆ ★

Knock, knock.
Who's there?
Wendy.
Wendy who?
Wendy red, red robin comes bob, bob, bobbing along…

★ ☆ ★

Knock, knock.
Who's there?
Whale.
Whale who?
Whale I'll be going back home since you're not opening the door.

★ ☆ ★

Knock, knock.
Who's there?
Whale.
Whale who?
Whale that certainly is a strange way to act.

★ ☆ ★

Knock, knock.
Who's there?
Whale.
Whale who?
I have a whale of a tale to tell you.

★ ☆ ★

Knock, knock.
Who's there?
Whale.
Whale who?
Whale, don't just stand there—open the door.

★ ☆ ★

Knock, knock.
Who's there?
Whale.
Whale who?
Open the door and I'll tell you a whale of a tale or two.

★ ☆ ★

Knock, knock.
Who's there?
Who.
Who who?
What are you—an owl?

★ ☆ ★

Knock, knock.
Who's there?
Why do owls go?
Why do owls go who?
Because that's the way they talk to each other.

★ ☆ ★

Knock, knock.
Who's there?
Wiggle.
Wiggle who?
Wiggle fall off if you don't use some glue.

★ ☆ ★

Knock, knock.
Who's there?
Winsome.
Winsome who?
Winsome, lose some.

★ ☆ ★

Knock, knock.
Who's there?
Wire.
Wire who?
Wire you always asking Who's there?

★ ☆ ★

Knock, knock.
Who's there?
Wooden shoe.
Wooden shoe who?
Wooden shoe like to know.

★ ☆ ★

Knock, knock.
Who's there?
Woodchuck.
Woodchuck who?
Woodchuck be able to come outside and play with us?

★ ☆ ★

Knock, knock.
Who's there?
Woody.
Woody who?
Woody please come up with better knock-knock jokes.

★ ☆ ★

Knock, knock.
Who's there?
Wound.
Wound who?
Wound you please let me in?

★ ☆ ★

Knock, knock.
Who's there?
X.
X who?
X, bacon, and toast are what I had for breakfast.

Sorry, Wrong Address!

Knock, knock.
Who's there?
Xs.
Xs who?
Xs me no questions and I'll tell you no lies.

★ ☆ ★

Knock, knock.
Who's there?
Xylophone.
Xylophone who?
Xylophone is a new phone you use to call Xylos.

★ ☆ ★

Knock, knock.
Who's there?
Yaw.
Yaw who?
Are you a cowboy?

Knock, knock.
Who's there?
Yoda.
Yoda who?
Yoda man.

★ ☆ ★

Knock, knock.
Who's there?
Yoga.
Yoga who?
Yoga any idea how tired I am of all these jokes?

★ ☆ ★

Knock, knock.
Who's there?
Yolanda.
Yolanda who?
Yolanda on your bottom when you fall down the stairs.

★ ☆ ★

Knock, knock.
Who's there?
You.
You who?
You-hoo, yourself.

★ ☆ ★

Knock, knock.
Who's there?
Yukon.
Yukon who?
Yukon come out here with me if you like.

★ ☆ ★

Knock, knock.
Who's there?
Yule.
Yule who?
Yule be laughing at this joke.

★ ☆ ★

Knock, knock.
Who's there?
Zany.
Zany who?
Zany body going to ever answer the door?

★ ☆ ★

Knock, knock.
Who's there?
Zeno.
Zeno who?
Zeno evil, hear no evil, speak no evil.

Other Books by Bob Phillips

All-Time Awesome Collection of Good Clean Jokes for Kids

The Awesome Book of Bible Trivia

The Awesome Book of Cat Humor

The Awesome Book of Dog Humor

The Awesome Book of Heavenly Humor

Awesome Good Clean Jokes for Kids

Awesome Knock-Knock Jokes for Kids

The Best of the Good Clean Jokes

Bible Trivia for Every Day

Dude, Got Another Joke?

Extremely Good Clean Jokes for Kids

Fabulous and Funny Clean Jokes for Kids

Flat-Out Awesome Knock-Knock Jokes for Kids

Good Clean Jokes to Drive Your Parents Crazy

Good Clean Knock-Knock Jokes for Kids

How Can I Be Sure?

How to Deal with Annoying People

A Joke a Day Keeps the Doctor Away

Jolly Jokes for Older Folks

Laughter from the Pearly Gates

Nutty Knock-Knock Jokes for Kids

Over the Hill & On a Roll

Over the Next Hill & Still Rolling

Over the Top Clean Jokes for Kids

Overcoming Anxiety and Depression

Super Incredible Knock-Knock Jokes for Kids

The World's Greatest Collection of Clean Jokes

The World's Greatest Knock-Knock Jokes for Kids

For more information, send a self-addressed stamped envelope to

Family Services
P.O. Box 9363
Fresno, California 93702